undercurrents

Also by Jane Williams and published by Ginninderra Press
Begging the Question
Parts of the Main
echoes of flight
Oskar Saves the World
My Nan Speaks Nanish
Points of Recognition

Jane Williams

undercurrents

Acknowledgements

Some of these poems were previously published in
The Canberra Times, *Island*, *Mona*, *StylusLit*.

'So much depends upon…' was shortlisted for the 2022 ACU Poetry Prize (Hope).

Thanks to the Southern Midlands Council for a residency in Oatlands, Tasmania.

Some of these poems were developed as part of the More Than Human Poetry Project initiated and facilitated by Kristen Lang.

For Ralph

undercurrents
ISBN 978 1 76109 565 8
Copyright © text Jane Williams 2023
Cover image: *Spring Light*, watercolour by Ron C. Moss

First published 2023 by
GINNINDERRA PRESS
PO Box 3461 Port Adelaide 5015
www.ginninderrapress.com.au

Contents

Cohabitation	7
As if nothing is wrong	8
Reach	10
Reckoning	11
Woman walking	13
Parallels	15
Meta	17
The hoons	18
Life skewed	19
First response	20
Mother tongues	21
Swan-knowledge	23
Waiting room	25
Pitstop	26
Matriline	27
Anomalies	29
Of a time	30
Confirmation	31
Rockface	33
Boy with bicycle pump	34
His day in the mall	35
Window of cloud	36
This terra form	37
Immersion	38
My mother tells another third-person story	39
So much depends upon…	40
Her Duckness	42
Bounty	44
Note to child-self	45
Aura	46

Accounting	48
In service	50
Rocky aka Veronica	52
La Niña	53
Extension	54
Revelations	56
Template	57
Walking in water	58
The closest I've come to flying is swimming	59
The fitful heart	60
Writer as Reader	61
Impromptu	62
Thinking about explaining artist in residence to my Irish Catholic father ex merchant seaman retired chicken farmer	63
Between cities	66
Taking the shot	67
Colouring in the day	69
This embroidered life	70
Tuesday Scrabble	72
Quiet notes for friends	74
Layers	75
My mother's daughter	76
Chiaroscuro	78
Instant gratification	79
Hum and fray	80
Sulphur	82
Thrum	84

Cohabitation

I research the level of humidity
required for the Never Never plant
to breathe indoors
observe the rain-slicked moves
suburban roofs make
angling riverward
walk paths cracked with winter-
greening, gardens overlapping fanciful
blueprints and all of it, all of us
root bound under layers of spheres:

tropo, strato, medo, thermo, exo…

I practise unpeopling my poems
in an effort to become more birdlike
riding currents of purified air
diving through mirrors
shaking the sun-
lit fish into bite-sized pieces.
In this state time itself
is no longer the enemy
but a generous benefactor;
consider the wonders
contained in each second –
230 beats of the honey bee's wings
300,000 kilometres of light.

As if nothing is wrong

I am drawn to the open-endedness
of early morning walks
flipside to evening ones programmed
for joining the dots of the day.

A neighbour's roller door lifts on blackbirds
foraging a week's worth of spring as if a week
could be their lot. How would they know?
How do any of us know?

Rowboats hyphenate the river and the sky
is a stratocumulus tease.

But for the stalling scent of jasmine
I might trip on a dislodged paver
collide with a cyclist rounding a blind corner.

Households unshutter, wake to routine
to-do lists laced with leftover dreaming.

Two joggers paused on the sidewalk could be
talking about any one of these very things

but as I pass, nothing I could have guessed at

*…when we were growing up if someone died in the bush
you'd say at least they were doing something joyful…*

These words trailing me home staying with me

as I deadhead hydrangeas, pull bread from the oven

check the calendar for missed days

think of my brother as he was before and after
his scattered cremains a compromise to the ungrantable
wish *just leave me to rot under the gum trees*

as I give in to a square of carpeted sunlight
curl there for a while catlike, as if nothing is wrong…

Reach

I reach for the empty water bottle caught in the branches of the she-oak. I do this mentally because I cannot risk climbing the safety fence, scrabbling down the embankment and up the tree, after the wet weather we've had, with the river raging below, with my dodgy hips. If I squint just as the sun hits the plastic I can almost embellish a chrysalis for a giant glasswing butterfly and if that sounds like I'm making light of things it's just that sometimes shifting the weight of the argument from one hemisphere of my brain to the other stops play, forcing a reset. So the most I can do in this moment is to mentally reach for the bottle. To hurl it back through time, past the moulding and mixing, the heating and drilling, back before black gold fevered and fractured our bonds. At home I retrieve the cup left out in the rain, stand at the kitchen sink willing myself to remember to taste the difference…

Reckoning

No white feather could ever shame him into killing
but he wished the Salvos had better prepared him
for the indiscriminate warring world.

He reckoned a tightly rolled sleeping bag
made the best place to park your bum in winter
if you were that smart, if you were that lucky

and without the right-sized boots, a box of band-aids
was worth its weight, equal to at least one square meal.

He reckoned he'd outrun the virus as far as he could
now he needed a rest and maybe a little torch
to read the racing pages by. Someone to talk to now and then.

He didn't ask for much and hoped his life would cast
the smallest possible shadow
if the past would just leave him be.

He tried to follow most of the ten commandments
most of the time.

A big believer in the truth
but if someone was intent on bullshitting him
he could bullshit right back with the best of them.

He reckoned he could spot a liar by the light
by the quality of the light in their eyes.

When he said *Out West* it was like
he was saying *Amen*.

Sure, he took a drink and a bet but he couldn't abide
a druggie or a bludger.

He reckoned the biggest problem with politics was party politics
the way it could unpeople the streets with the stroke of a pen.

He cried out by way of salutation *No War!*
Spent the better part of each day waiting for echoes.

Woman walking

It begins with a woman's measured steps.

Not your steps, you are the observer seated
at a picnic table perhaps or one of those benches
overlooking the pond
– an unrefined Monet of harmonies
where the occasional rat floats among lily pads
and black and white Muscovy ducklings
are living their best feral lives.

It is too early, too cool yet for the takeover
of the families of small children.

The walking woman traverses back and forth
the length of the park.

Each stride of her cane-aligned leg seems at odds
with the other giving over to little mid-air shakes
as if trying to tease its own way, to break out
Charlie Chaplin style
transforming elder woman to ageless entertainer
walking stick to trademark prop
tapping and twirling
hooking villains and saving the merely
nearly drowned.

Now stopping to check the wristwatch
which is really a new age wellness portal
recording beats of the heart, calories burned
if not the choreography of original dance steps
if not the actual force by which the tide is slowed.

Now starting again completely unlost
in creaturely habit. And again.

Something about the white sunhat and gloves
has fashioned a reward smile
across the raw material of your morning.

At some point you notice   or don't
that whatever problem you brought to the park
has also mutated into manageable bite-sized
spitball pieces.

How much lighter for instance you feel
at the sight of the steel pole and bracket
supporting the cracked limb of a tree.

Ditto blossom caught in a spiderweb.

Also, that moment much later

when the image
of the walking woman has faded but lingers
like the discontinued perfume of an itinerant lover

when if asked
you could only truly describe yourself as a struck match

when someone long dead sends you a friend request
and you are almost born-again.

Parallels

A second pathogen-driven winter.
Who can bear it, putting faces to numbers?

The wet will not let up long enough
for a masked walk and world news is
a fickle rainbow, still each day we are
drawn forth, one life form among millions.

Honeyeaters wait out bare branches.
Spotted doves line telephone wires proving
paths of least resistance.
Magpies sing undaunted weaving their unifying
notes through our layers of mood.
Blooms of moss thread themselves
along garden paths celebratory as any bouquet.

All life has thirst in common.
Even the kangaroo rat adapted to live without
needs what little moisture the seed offers up.
The water-holding frogs and thorny devils trap
and store what they can.

Parallels abound.

Altruism and empathy in rats.
The underground network of trees.
Soprano purple daisies expanding
morning into afternoon.

And putting the size of the human brain
into perspective, the resilience of the
tardigrade / water bear / moss piglet.

Still we are counted.
We are counted among these marvels.

How does the world never tire of giving us
these chances?

What is the *more* we long for?

Meta

I do not understand the bread machine.
Metal paddle, timer, whir of motor.
Inbuilt memory, blackout survivor
steaming through the exhaust vent.

Ask me about bouquet and I might suggest
Journey to the Centre of the Earth
or if pushed for time hint at brine
laced with secondary notes of carbon
but I cannot speak to weights and measures
to military precision.

I am the runt of that litter.

What draws me in is this stretch and fold
frivolous and reverential
as one hundred strokes of hair the night before
the shave.

Each time I retrieve a fully formed loaf
from the feverish oven I am rewarded
by its alchemy, by how all that tries to dissuade
and disconnect me is paused and altered somehow –
the way this poem once written twice read
becomes less and less about bread.

The hoons

Once winked as the silver spoon
of immoral earnings
the century turned and turned again
until hooning became synonymous with
burnouts and fishtails legislated out
of the purely vernacular
encouraging citizens to report
(13hoon)

but mostly we never
saw the point.

Sleep deprived, beyond anger
we would simply give in to wondering
what they found in their cloud
of smoke in the reverberating night –
these caged souls chasing their own tails
through our suburban dreaming.
In their wake a friction of intersecting
circles to be continued…

How worrisome the concept
of peace must have been to them.
How fearful the great reveal
of silence.

Life skewed

A young man, fuzzy at the edges troubled by
dreams of disappearing altogether briefly took
up the pen and went into battle. Armed only
with unrequited love poems he pummelled
the plains with hyperbole but nothing grew
nothing grew back. One day soon after
he stopped taking his meds, then took them all.
At the debriefing, we whose job it was to help
make life bearable, joyful even sat around
the table like fallen knights bested
by invisible dragons.

*

My aunt returned from a routine grocery shop
and although she had the right key and a good
enough marriage could not re-enter the house
because the weight of the body of my dead uncle
blocked the way. It is a piece of family history
I learn matter-of-factly, still I find myself cornered
by the comparative horrors of husband and wife.

*

I rationalise these two deaths
side by side, generations and oceans apart
signifies nothing more than encoding
storage and retrieval but what else is the mind
doing if not striving to connect with the heart
with the potential of soul
that conciliatory window always opening on life
skewed in favour of life.

First response

Just a few inches of water
in the bottom of a fire
bucket. Concentric circles
see me placing my trust
back in search engines.
Physics is just
one more thing I do
not understand
though I get that googling
everything is reductive.
I am close to believing
each year's resolution
is tested by disaster
by virtue of our response
to counterfeit lives.
Wishing is not the same
as praying but take pity
on our desperation
tossing coins in a pail
in the hope of returning
to cities clean and eternal
and not of our making.

Mother tongues

Monolingual I can only eavesdrop
with my imagination.
Can only guess wrongly at most languages.
Take this one on the other side
of the corrugated iron
separating factory from garden.
The tone chatty, communal
news and ideas exchanged
at high-pitched breakneck speed.
Where one sentence, one topic
begins and ends I am ill-equipped to tell.
Could the dullness of my own
mother tongue hold such appeal?
Like a child wondering at the other side
of the mirror I stare at what I cannot see
enthralled by overlapping voices
punctuated with shared laughter
and the occasional English phrase:
an excited drawn-out
Oh   my   God
the practised cheer of
Good morning sir.
Little mannered peacekeepers
and hints at personality:
can you please sorry sorry
your country my country
ah this song this one
exactly exactly OK OK…

At one point I press my ear
to warm metal as if by feeling
the vernacular's vibration
I might comprehend more.
That night my friend alerts me to the quicksand
of unearned leaps and bounds in poetry
which leads me to thinking
about superpowers in general and
X-ray vision in particular. As if tomorrow
I might be capable of staring down a wall
to reveal those parts of the human body
soundlessly communicable:
shrug of shoulder wink of eye curl of lip
passed down from dream-weaving hearts
quickening minds mother to daughter
calloused hand to calloused hand…

Swan-knowledge

We have taken to following the locals along the rivulet
next to the golf course, a daily check-in on the nesting swan.
Rising floodwaters (we know from a mythology of experience)
will be eclipsed soon enough by burning bushes.
We count eggs diligently – one, two, three…
all the way up to five.

The weave of sticks intact though a little farther from the bank
a little testy at the edges. In its centre this broody life
blackly feathered, all unmet hunger and questioning neck
now and then redistributing weight but staying the distance.
Staying put. How do they do it? How do we not?

Sparrows flit in and out of latticework like so much Disney.
As if happy endings are written into every contract.
What else? Oh, the snatched breath each time an ivory flash
in the reeds turns out to be a golf ball.

At some point we start adding to our bank of swan-knowledge.
We learn about moulting, how it renders them earthbound
for weeks on end, marvel at the energy it must take
to grow enough new feathers to survive another winter.
Discover they were hunted to extinction in some parts
allegedly tasting like roast beef, ask ourselves why
we find this disturbing, suddenly dreaming
of cows as sacrosanct.

When four out of five hatch, the delight is palpable.
We stop short of congratulating ourselves.
What did we have to do with any of it after all?

But once the countdown begins, reaching all the way back
to one, it is as if some grievous wrong has been committed
on our watch. And for a while we nick each other
with the incomplete rawness of our greetings
retreat to the controlled substance of our lives
once more tending to our own, real or imagined
newly celebrated or mourned. Those of us who recall
the fairy tale warnings, resume the counting of children
the sidelong glances into small faces, alert to the vaguest
changeling sign. Is it forgivable to say we never felt
quite so alive?

Waiting room

In its centre a man standing holding court
royally oblivious to the rest of us
wall-flowered behind masks
each chair a chair-width apart.
Our private silent vigils above reproach.

His phone on loud speaker he follows the echo
of his wife's instructions to look first in pockets;
jacket (outside and in) trousers (back and front)
to breathe, to think, to not worry
and finally…there!
Inside the shopping bag on the tray of
the walking frame he favours like a dog
with a nose for home.

He doesn't need our permission
has no need to imagine us in our underwear.

How many times has he shrunk to its nub
a moment like this one?
Each time guided by her voice, even now
age-thinned, almost spectral.

We dare not roll our eyes for fear they betray
our own weak spots, our quiet longings
to be oh so known.

Pitstop

Abandoned now but once
a pitstop for families on road trips
midway point between home and
elsewhere ramping up the testy
mantra *are we there yet?*
and I wish the memories stopped at
bowsers pumping up pipe dreams
sticky fingers and 10 green bottles but
I keep thinking about that phone call.
You asking if you could visit and
stay, telling me there'd been a
road accident, that the truckie walked
away but not her, she was dead and
while they said it would have been instant
painless, you can't get it straight in your
head and your heart is in peril because
one of the last things you talked about
together was whispered in lover-speak.
Asked what you would do if she ever
left, you said you'd follow, you promised
you'd follow…

Matriline

Longevity and adaptation run through my matriline
and I cannot say which is the cause, which the effect.
Just that we keep on keeping on to the chime of
grandfather clocks, to the call of the cuckoo.
Smiles like black market nylons stretched across
generations. Chickens feature in a disjointed way.
The kindred spirits of cows. I embellish at least
as much as I know. It could be my superpower.
In the beginning at the end of the first warring
world forming muscle memory and a knack
for lucid dreaming, those lucky enough not to draw
the short straw as a canary girl in munitions kept
going until they reached the first unfettered
movements of domestic sovereignty: tresses
carpeting salon or kitchen floors, poems candidly
listing affairs like occasion dresses. Fleeing now
and then to the sky or the sea. Intuition always
a microsecond ahead of the starter's gun
sprinting between the lines before the dust settled
once more over not quite everything. Not the telephone
for instance, harbinger of inception and termination.
Of reinvention. Coding serious intent through tattle.
Discerning wrong numbers from infidelities. I used it
once to announce I would be wearing the empire-waist
in off-white; ignoring my mother's advice that he was
too young for the part, for both parts. Then the first time
he left. Then the second time he left. Without the aid of
matchmakers what is there to consider but the force of
the spark? Had she warned me against the escape artists
I only would have found them sooner. Thumbing rosary beads

– they love me, they love me not. Gravitating to backdoors
trapdoors, souped-up revs, high-octane kisses. Drowning in
the shallows and mishearing each time they swore hand on
heart black and blue – I am just so in lust with you baby I
could cry. When I could not stop my sister and mother
from outliving their sons, I found anything else for my hands
to do. Stockpiling wood and wool. Lacing tobacco. Soaking
new stains. Dyeing old ones. Setting an extra place – needing
to believe I was God's favourite, that we are all some god's
favourite. We keep on and if imagination has anything to do
with it, let us imagine this: granddaughters sourcing feathers
from the imagined Book of Phoenix, chewing frankincense
gum open-mouthed, painting eyelids gold or sapphire –
little flame-throwers intent on life. For as long as we are able
let us cheer from the sidelines, sometimes join in –
apprentice to their warble and shimmy, their deeper respect
for wishbones.

Anomalies

That year sleep was a thief and I was on guard.
At school camp, I claimed the night all night
in the common room taunting the asthmatic fire.

The boy I wanted, who did not want me
(not exactly, not publicly) declined my invitation
on a coin toss, retreating to adolescent ridicule.

Earlier that afternoon when I pointed out
the day moon to no one in particular
he slowed his step to match mine just long enough to ask
if I'd thought of becoming some kind of artist
and because I was a little in love with him
and with the moon
I weighted his question disproportionally.

I do not wonder now how things might have
panned out (upturning heads instead of tails).
The night was anomalous but we were
pigeon-holed with only our stereotypes
in common: his calculated life
mine of relative impulse.
How vigilance checked him.
How shadow play unearthed me.

I was no more surprised to hear
that he enlisted than he would have been
to learn I turned that night into a poem
between breaths between sleeps
my mind's eye never fully closing again.

Of a time

Once more unearthed, this wedding polaroid
flaunting brazen youth and rumoured knowing:
which aunt to hug, which uncle to avoid,
your wry grin, the cliché of my glowing.
Time has healed enough to say we meant
each vow, each wink, each rendered way of being.
Those days were music, passion fuelled and spent,
betrayal's warning signs unheard, unseen.
Like lovers through the ages, we were one but
playing house revealed a different stroke –
windows, doors, then hearts began to shut.
As if a spell reversed itself, we woke.
Put simply, we were right and then were wrong.
It's just a photo loyal to a song.

Confirmation

This morning rediscovering
a book unthought of
since well before lockdown
became a household name
randomly opening
at a poem about chance
earmarked
by two flowering stems
of undeclared
bog cotton.

Flipping through
to further come upon
clover cuttings pressed
between the pages.
Instinctively I pause
to count each leaf.

Such slight things
to smuggle home
back in the day
when touch was still
a welcome form
of confirmation.

What was I thinking?

That there may come a time
when demarcation of family
was the natural order
and travel the sport of daredevils?

These tufts, so featherlike.
These pale green trios
still veiny
against all expectation.

Rockface

Though one will swear rabbit
the other wombat...
aware of the true nature
of the animal-shaped rock
the couple in the parked car
sipping tea from the shared flask
show the same interest ask
the same questions
as if it were the real thing:
diet, shelter, predators (natural and not)
and the barb – that left to its wildness
how would they know any fancy from fact?

Later they will lighten the mood with wordplay:
sedentary and sedimentary
noc and rock turnal
but at the time
each on the verge of confessing
from the corner of the eye a spied movement
a twitch, something to indicate existence was rife
a colony if not wisdom   life imitating life.

Boy with bicycle pump

Outside the antique shop
the boy with the bicycle pump
paces and circles
the few square feet of pavement
he's been instructed to wait upon
and where holiday boredom
soon becomes metamorphic
as he finds himself (still just young enough)
to be wielding at turns:
a root digger, leaf blower,
muscle builder (shoulders, chest and back)
tree lopper, walking cane
a throwing stick in search of a dog
briefly a sword but at no point a gun
and just once eyes half-closed
the quintessential magic wand
creating a vortex into which the last vestiges
of childhood may one day but not today
vanish before our unbelieving eyes.

His day in the mall

Last day of school break clutching the hand of his date
a teenage boy walking through town radiates conviction
as if against all odds he truly earned his day in the mall
with the popular girl.
Each line, each move, doggedly rehearsed into fact.
How credible he looks, hair flicked and freeze-framed
clothes on-trend. But his wayward smile is debunking
the grave tone of his voice on the phone as he whispers
I'm in hospital, had a bad reaction to…and then he is gone
dissolved by the holiday crowd of wannabees
just far enough away from wherever he is meant to be.
And what of the girl by his side – complicit in the falsehood?
So taken by his public persona I confess to not properly seeing her
but I understand the game; playing at being colour-blind
willing red and green to mean the same sure thing
the relative worth of a spring day honeyed with lies.

Window of cloud

Entering my fifty-seventh year
Perseverance touches down on Mars
as earth's pandemics continue, as I continue
spared by little more than x marking
the smallest spot on the map
of the world, of my body.

My window
of cloud offers up a frayed blue
hole of sky, its déjà vu comfort
is palpable.

The tidal river below is postcard-flat.
Rows of furled masts infinitely patient
their shadows merely alluding to depth
while down at the marina, boats
rally their 'fix the mud' signs.

It seems the more we try to sculpt
the earth the more she digs in her heels
insists on going her own way.

In the middle distance, sporadic traffic
corrugated rooftops.
From every reflective surface
the sun blinks an ancient morse code
only our DNA remembers.

This terra form

for KL

As predicted my gaze is sharpened and lifted
by the fog's slow reveal, by all I know and
hope to be extant beyond the Golden Arches:

gilded veins of gum leaves

eyeless worms sensing
the same light differently.

Morning unfolds like a faded love note
I remember verbatim before and after
its author.

Huxley's island birds still call for attention
when I think of them

but here it's the magpies who cajole me
into being
into inhabiting my terra form more or less
authentically that is to say intentionally
placing my trust in life's ellipsis
in blooms of jellyfish older than dinosaurs.

Immersion

As observers we are ever in danger
of drowning in a mythology of colour.

Hercules walking his dog for instance
a sea snail held in the maw
canine drool purpling the sand.

Then there's the question of
procurement, of sovereignty –

how much mucus did it take
to dye the robes of royalty

the single stripe permitted
in a senator's toga?

We might think oh to be born into purple
and its wealth of limitations

but doesn't life always ask more?
An invitation to participate, to face

its magnetic storm of what ifs; contribute
to the warp and weft of this moment
of whatever comes next…

My mother tells another third-person story

…this one about a washerwoman pegging patterns
of colour to signal a neighbour the coast is clear
for unravelling into each other's keeping
all their stored-up words of the week.

I imagine them midway through
their shared hero's journey holding hands
at the threshold of the inmost cave.
But I only imagine this. I do not know if she
is merely the teller of the story
its protagonist or antagonist
only that it is a tale old as nettle pudding
glazed over with a veneer of domesticities:
the importance of a well-oiled back door
money in your own name
a small but serviceable suitcase
etiquette honed over untameable yearnings.

I am passing on my version of such narratives
to daughters and granddaughters who will
correct me on certain points of (r)evolution.

When the newest member of our women's
poetry group says quietly *I am a they*
before staggering us with a reading
about reptilian allure
I feel the holes in every backstory
illuminate into portals of wonder.

Weeks later I find myself
hanging out the washing wearing
a circus hat, on the verge of breaking
into uncoded song.

So much depends upon…

Today the fog cancels all flights in and out.
The city (in name only) hugs itself back through time
to the unparcelled land it was dreamed on.

Could this be what is happening to me?

All I did was breathe and a tiny cloud formed
inside my left breast behind my newly inverted nipple.
Such a soft landing it almost went unnoticed.
How strange, how intimate, this climate change.

Textbooks are rife with the grim humour
of oxymorons

small mass   simple mastectomy

My sister curses on my behalf
and I love her for it.
We message back and forth into the night;
crude jokes crossing the line, hitting
and (in this version) obliterating the spot.

I decide to fatten up beaver-like for winter
though we are almost midway through.
Closable ears could also come in handy
(one less evil to admit to)
but for now the fattening up will do
perhaps a few basic lessons in damming.
In damning.

The Red Wheelbarrow has always convinced me
less is more but really so much else depends upon
genetics, lifestyle and the gusto of a coin toss;
on being born into a certain century
part of the world, side of the tracks.

My daughter introduces me to Yuko Hosaka.
A woman superimposed over a bird in flight and
I am in love all over again choosing to believe
that a work of art so flatly multidimensional
means anything is possible.

My newest grandchild is calmed by bachata –
her parents dance before her with each other as if
welcoming the first citizen of the new world.

Friends remind me of the circumspection
of medics, the favourable weight of statistics.
Countable/uncountable all the women
whose stories make room for mine.
I place an each-way bet, dare to call it prayer
reassure myself
there are questions no one has asked that only I
(surely) can answer.

The poem's title is taken from 'The Red Wheelbarrow' by William Carlos Williams.

Her Duckness

I keep returning to the dabblers
divers and perchers
after an overheard snippet
between women
riffling through trinkets
in a second-hand shop
sighing their ancient sighs.
One proclaiming
everything covid related
had dulled her impulse for travel;
she will not visit the family
this year if ever again, lamenting
I am tired of it all now.
The other, sympathetic
leaning in as women have always done
sharing advice, gossip, common sense
solutions to world problems...
Do you know what you need?
Ducks. They will help. Ducks, ducks ducks!

I hear that and wonder in what way
they might help, these ducks.
The pragmatist suspects
Christmas panic buying
and an early sell out on turkeys
but the dreamer is courting
that other kind of comfort
found in the philosophies
of Leunig cartoons.

More meaningful than
whispered nothings
tickling auriculars
or even navigation by the stars –
this unanimous vote
favouring short legs
and depressed bodies.
Her venerable duckness
finally assured
of being picked for the team.

Bounty

There was a time I couldn't get enough
of the great birds:
the thrill of any raptor mid-hunt
the hypnotic swank of a fanning peacock.
My flying dreams were epic
gulls and pigeons demoted to sidekicks.
For so long I was unable or unwilling to acknowledge
the Cher Amis and Jonathan Livingstons
to appreciate the minutiae of a life's work
the delicacy of skeletons that leave no trace.

These days I strive to be a woman who can sit
among winged rats
unaware of the measure of time –
face unfolding, downsizing its wide
accommodating smile to *sfumato*
mind rewinding to now
all desire quelled by breath's bounty
by the elemental company of human whisperers…

Note to child-self

Remember the blood-warmth of the sun
aligning your senses. Remember a frisson
of days leaping from one nerve end to the next.
Remember your sap chewing, nectar sipping self.
Remember climbing trees, reading in trees, being
swayed by trees. Remember your rapport with
collared dogs, harnessed horses, any caged and
spirited thing. Remember holding shell after shell
to your ear listening for your whispered name
in the ocean's memoir. Remember how the rain
that kept you indoors rewarded with its
thrumming song against the window and the roof
then later with puddles and streams, how the world
glistened and you with it, the visceral comfort
of your mingling scents. Remember the rhythmic
stability of the moon remembering you…

Aura

Between torrents, news reports of unlikely heroes
but also hooning through floodwaters
reckless as tourist-bravado in snake season
unwilling to settle for mere kangaroos in the mall.
Why should this day, fine enough for walking –
the vaporous air spiked with eucalypt and wattle –
be any different?
Before I reach the graffitied rockface and city views
the overblown rivulet and big little waterfall
a silent alarm lowers my line of sight to the hand
of the first teenage girl emerging
from the 100-metre drop then her companion
following move for move hands hauling
elbows, torsos, knees. Reassembling the status quo.
As if they were only ever marionettes waiting
after some choreographed fall, to rise again.
By the time they are standing we are close enough
to register each other's adrenalin
the guilty pleasures of risk and of witness.
Strands of hair stripe flushed faces and everything
about them pulses in the aftermath of near miss.
If I believed in auras, if I believed I could see auras
theirs might be orange with hard-learned lessons
or pure joy depending which reference book you use.
If they were cats, I'd wonder which life they were on.
Of course, I cannot tell them anything
they do not think they already know.
I do not even ask why. For they are in the age of falling
and rising water and blood exacting acts of God.

Rejecting anything by rote.
They leave as they came; barefoot, unharnessed
alive for now in that fluky middle ground between death
by misadventure and leaving a note.

Accounting

Over chicken wonton soup, talk of retirement
after toeing someone else's line or even
a job loved, self-made, superbly done

then someone says

being an artist must be like
living your never-ending passion like
living your best life.

I can't speak for the others:
the painters and dockers and sculptors
the singers and social workers and dancers
the potato-farming playwrights…

or how any of us will account for days
that simply run into each other
clocking on and off, indifferent
to neurons misfiring efforts
to resist the good old tropes, the softer sell
when every idea seems booby trapped
each manifestation chipped or cracked.

But yes
there are other, finer times; on the brink
for instance, of taking up another trade
when someone else admits to reading poetry
out loud to their gastroenterologist whose approval
restores faith in the science of daydreaming
lighting up the brain's executive net.

We are worthy those days for sure
maybe even as close to our true selves
as we're likely to get
though we can't say quite how we got there
or if we will ever return. Just that we are
simultaneously adrift and firing on all pistons –
part mermaiden, part super buoy, watching
awestruck, the eelgrass grow, preserving shipwrecks
spring-cleaning and breathing
through our deepest blues.

In service

i.m. Stephen Dunn poet 1931–2021

Some of us it's true, get to meet our heroes and walk through
the rest of our lives spurred on in part by some photograph
or signature, contact's enduring imprint, the dream intact.

For others it's the blunt end of disappointment as if
the real thing is too much like waking to daytime dimness
after childhood's canopy of glow-in-the-dark stars.

I could not fathom meeting you outside the poem and this
was your gift.

When someone said here read this and handed me one of your books
I couldn't get enough of your bare-boned seeing. At a dinner party
I held court reading about that school reunion or was it
the parable of the tiger raised by goats? The silence that followed
fed us too. We were past the age of certainty and any other night
might have settled for the tablecloth trick. So, thank you for
what goes on.

I won't pretend I revelled in everything you wrote or that
there weren't times I felt a little let down by how cleverly and
necessarily you removed yourself from the rest (of us).

But I am grateful you weren't the right kind of famous for
a tabloid reveal and it would be accurate (though not nearly enough
of a tribute) to say there were more days than not when your poems
breathed for me, resetting the clock, humbling illuminations
on the good service of love's grist. On happy friends
who don't read poetry, finding it instead in the way
the couch yields to their shape after the end of a working week
and the dog or cat or small child seem to sigh ah all's right
with our world now you're home now you're home...

What goes on is the title of Stephen Dunn's Selected and new poems 1995–2009, W.W. Norton, 2009.

Rocky aka Veronica

When we move in you are already ensconced
sunbathing next to the rockery
soaking up the heat from the asphalt path
leading to the front door. As good looking
a blotched blue-tongue as ever there was.
I fall in love with you in slow-motion.
Like any hobbyist who fancies themselves
a true aficionado, like any Hollywood name
dropper worth their salt or rather, someone else's
I proclaim your attributes in selective company:
The tongue's royal hue. Suits of camouflage
routinely shed. Predators hoodwinked by your
escaped tail. You woo me with the word brumation.
Then there's that third eye atop your head
distinguishing day from night, night from day.
You appear and disappear and each time
I am a little afraid you have succumbed
to a backlash of cats and dogs
to snail bait or that you have somehow
been jinxed by the arrogance of my naming you.
I make seasonal offerings: fresh organic strawberries
saucers of hailstones…

La Niña

Everything burgeoning
closing in on its use-by date.
Still the naturalists walk the rivulet
outfitted for preservation
waterproof jackets and protective gloves
rubbish bags and pick-up sticks.
At some point they find themselves debating
colour; not the ripening hues of landscape
already coined by army camouflage
Desert Sand Urban Grey Foliage Green
but rather the exact shade
of a newly hatched cygnet.
Maybe no one actually says
darker than the sun's core or
lighter than moon dust but
surely someone is recalling
the blown dandelions of their childhood
Rumpelstiltskin spinning. Thinking
first Champagne, last cigarette.
And isn't everyone touched
just a little by the odd
rats and ravens, unrestrained dogs…

Extension

From one hundred disused acres of memory
this one; a rented farmhouse, two daughters
more than a few cats and chickens
a dam my visiting mother dared to swim in
an almost antique Olivetti typewriter.

How one morning the decision to clean
the gutters instead of the oven, restored me.

Balancing on corrugated panels
bending to scoop fallen leaves – bend scoop bend scoop –
did I learn this from the wind?
The ensuing feeling of wellness in the few still
moments after the act, standing there on the roof.
Aluminium channels clear of debris.
Muscles aching with the pleasure of autonomous use
of being without clarification.

Looking out across the vegie patch
to the chook house, the winding dirt road I had yet
to learn to drive. I was not thinking then
only now thirty years on
about the inevitable lot
of stray cats, cancerous roosters.
Which version of the truth to tell children.
How much longer, how much farther
my mother might have swum without her husband
looking on.

How my typewriter was once used
by a court reporter
and what the ghost in the machine
in any machine might have to teach
any one of us about connectivity
and embodiment on the rickety cusp
of the year of the rat.

Revelations

The first time I read to a round table of strangers
so long ago now I can't recall the details of faces
only that we ranged spanning generations and dispositions
from the barefaced to the barely there.
Ratty notebooks edged in wordless doodles.
Sheets of A4 typed and spring-clipped to attention.
It was as if we were waiting our turn to be interviewed
for jobs we didn't want or bank loans we did.

A single poem folded and tucked into the back pocket
of my jeans gave me the option to pass

but the teenager's angst was my own all too recently
to easily dismiss the chinked armour of sisterhood
and the old woman's nostalgia was a house
that could not be blown down
and the wide-eyed man's slow-winding story
about a trial lover who'd stayed over
waking to a kitchen of stale bread and spoiled milk
showed promise.

Levelled by our desire to be seen through
our montage of words
exquisite little shards of fairy-taled mirror
never quite as prophetic or vital again.

Template

after *El Camino de Esmeralda* by Danelle Rivas

Some selves are easier to reimagine…
Let me begin by admitting I am no seamstress
that I must rely in part on eye-catching design
and the kindness of elves.
How to costume a life in the midst of living?
Selection is everything and nothing –
one memory weaves a picture the next unpicks.
What to keep and what to swap out?
Unblinking how easily a flag unpatterns itself.
A train becomes a ship, fallopian tubes waving
off passengers from port to port.
Tropical flowers give way to golden wattles and
shamrocks, if I go back far enough maybe
a tiny white bulb pushing through Viking snow.
I give the lizard a blue tongue encircling
the first strawberry of summer.
The hummingbird becomes a fairy wren
wish-whispering in my ear cautioning
trekking through the mindscape alone.
My mouth is hidden behind a bouquet of half-truths
but see here what my hands offer up:
beneath a therapy of pets, the roar of the poem.

Walking in water

You could never call me a strong swimmer.
I still hold my nose jumping into the deep
and have not mastered
any proper technique for breathing.
But like the sun along any horizon
I find myself drawn to all manner of aqua
from bathtubs to whirlpools
forecast rain, unscripted tears
scattered light after skipped pebbles.
My movements become undulated and
interchangeable. I dream of flying
through great tidal waves and
find as much comfort in the word nimbostratus
as in the way the new woman at the local pool
holds to its edge, sidestepping
up and down the shallows before letting go
one finger at a time.
Who says she is only interested in learning
how to walk in water. The rest, she is sure
will take care of itself…

The closest I've come to flying is swimming

The closest I've come to flying is swimming,
submerging myself again and again.
Are the chambers of my heart inflating?

So much dross falls away when I'm floating.
Perhaps we all end up where we began.
The closest I've come to flying is swimming.

One day I'll master circular breathing,
attuning my sonic pulse to each plane
with the chambers of my heart inflating.

Weightless, each movement a new beginning,
the spaces between the strokes guide the way.
The closest I've come to flying is swimming.

Buoyed by the sound of the cosmos singing,
what if someone calls me in from my lane,
stops the chambers of my heart inflating?

Between here and there stars are dimming,
but collective dreams and memory remain.
The closest I've come to flying is swimming.

The less life I have the more I'm living.
Nobody needs to remember my name,
I've come so close to flying through swimming
the chambers of my heart are inflating.

The fitful heart

Though the boy is still a boy
when he learns
about the fitful heart
about death and the odds
against beating it;
his engineer-father there
one minute explaining
the difference between ohm and om
and the problem of the travelling salesman
…gone the next and the next…
he believes if he just keeps
showing up
with a ready smile and
a dogsbody willingness
to please, keeps turning
the other cheek sooner
rather than later
he will have earned acceptance
if not respect and something else
some palatable facsimile of love.

Writer as Reader

Raised on a mixed bag of
classicpopfictionhardcorebiblicalpaperbacks
bookended by Shakespeare and Sherlock
my tastes grew on the fly, elastic if not eclectic.

To the extent that my writing is the product
of my reading it would be prudent to say
I was at different stages both lover
and fair-weather friend to the Word.

I picked up rhythm and humour
from Banjo and Pam.

My angst and longing from Sylvia and Leonard.

E.D. and E.E. showed me the only way out
was to keep my head slant and low.

I discovered
the hard work sophistication could be.
Easy slide of wit and wordplay.
The lonely exclusivity of difficult poetry.

There were times I dabbled in the grave until
the light grew almost too weak to dig by.

The simple truth is I never outgrew
The Faraway Tree. I'm still there
perched on its uppermost branch
head in the ether, anticipation being
the other half of the sum
of all provocations yet to come.

Impromptu

Having allowed her hair to whiten and drift
past neck's pseudo strength
the shrug shoulders are schooled to unlearn
trailing spine's curve
through an alphabet of growth spurts
to rest at that sweet spot where
another's hand once and perhaps still
harbours itself in dance,

even a cautious woman can reach an age
and find herself among strangers
making small talk but thinking of Yeats
sailing to Byzantium
and encouraged by autumn's gilded light
spontaneously recite the final stanza.

So it is then that we are drawn in, captured
by the quiet command of an unlikely voice.
The quiver of a lower lip, beyond lovely.

Our own body language looser than we
remember being possible, faces unchecked.
Our reptilian brains unknowingly feeding
on beat and stress, pitch and timbre –
a rhythmic fluidity she is choosing to share
eyes focussed elsewhere all the while
gifting us this deeply personal
invitation to follow at our own shy pace.

Thinking about explaining artist in residence to my Irish Catholic father ex merchant seaman retired chicken farmer

I was always going to be a maker, Dad, the question was only ever
whether I would make paint or paintings, money or poems
loaves of bread or pints of stout.
How else to measure an honest day's work if not by what you put into it
what others get out…
This convict-built town once boasted seven hotels *(do I have your attention now?)*.
Its inhabitants reach back and forward pulled between ancestral memory
and new age vision.
I don't mean for this to be about that or even about you
(watch what you say
to that one it might end up in a book).
But then how can I help it when I feel connected at every turn…
just yesterday, reading about the nationalist sent here for treason
who doctored from the cottage across the way.
And today didn't I meet a woman who accents as far north as yourself
and bears my very own name? So of course I had to tell her you're not long back
from visiting the old country, on the heels of Covid, all 92 mulish years of you
(that I didn't say).

Then there's Easter which has all but passed and I have yet to set foot
in my Father's house.
Anzac Day badges selling on one corner and roosters escaping around the next.
But back to the why of it all...
Perhaps it would make more sense to talk about the view or the climate
but I have to tell it my own way –
breathing in the pigmented molecules of the past mood swings of past artists
caught off guard by the light weight bearing of ceiling hooks and hanging wire
this wooden work table on wheels, the way every corner holds an easel, the way
heritage sandstone and wallpaper hold me briefly just so in the very act of making
this poem even as I seem to be doing little more than staring out the shopfront window
wool gathering, wondering about the half road closed sign, the trapdoor that creaks
underfoot, the giant key that only locks from outside. And in a nod to pragmatism
the past few weeks have seen me bartering poetry and bread for chocolate, apples
and coffee, a virtual tour of Florence, a glimpse into the serious side of astrology and
the building blocks of Russian art.

It's all grist for the mill, even the starlings in the roof and the
 mice in the walls
which I know would drive you to despair. It might seem like
 malarkey but I come by it
honestly so *there, there Dad there, there…*

Between cities

Between cities these midland towns
where old-fashioned meets new-fangled
and colonial silhouettes just one side of the story.

It used to be that Off Season meant
a girl could ride her horse
and a man could walk his sheep
down the main street without turning a head.
Now it's year-round tourists and burst border bubbles.

Young couples pull up campervans lakeside
testing their newfound belief in each other
sure they've got what it takes to be without
anyone else.

From their motorhomes with add-ons
the grey nomads smile benignly and place
a quiet bet.

Café owners order in more nut milk
than they can shake a stick at, make sure
there's gluten free vegan options on the menu.

The imagined view from the other side
pulls this way and that.
Some days the temptations must be equally great –
to stay and be counted or break free from the pack.

Taking the shot

I know a little about walking around ladders
sidestepping cracks
keeping butter fingers away from mirrors
and other vanities

though admit to sometimes wilfully
forgetting
whether it's bad or good luck
to have a black cat cross your path.

And now this
perfectly formed rabbit
materialising in the pre-dawn autumn chill
just ahead of me.
Barking dogs a distant threat.
Composition and contrast
promisingly evocative.

Here for the images and
the poems they may engender
I reach for my camera (old school)
rendering the scene instantly
static.

No subject was ever stiller
and at this point I am tempted
to thank my model for posing
so compliantly
but the part of me that knows better
knows worse.

Indistinguishable to some
– camera and gun –
and though I take the shot
with minimal motion
I know it's after-image I'll live with
beyond beauty the terrified heart
of *Oryctolagus cuniculus*
the unaccountable beats.

Colouring in the day

It might be possible
to warm up a little
by taking in the vibrancy
of the free-ranging rooster's
Imperial comb
the Firebrick vintage
parked down the road
the dabbling Candy Apple
beaks of the swans;
all of which I'm sure to pass
on my brisk morning walk.

But before that
there's something to be said
for just turning up the heat
and continuing to gaze
through this particular window
at the way, for instance
the light is catching just now
(despite or because of
a heavily overcast day)
the Tuscan Sun of the earring
worn by the woman
dressed in Fuchsia alighting
the Chartreuse car
a fluffy Simply White cloud
(vaguely dog-shaped)
underarm.

This embroidered life

If midday is the yardarm for a tipple
what is it for chocolate?
Is 8.45 a.m. too early to crack open
that Toblerone I have hidden in the kitchen
inside a rodent-proof box?
Excuse enough perhaps that the unpredicted
rain has arrived pulling the sky down
so low I feel as though I could reach up
and with one finger scrawl a message
across its vast ashen face…
But what to say that isn't merely more
of the same   *Have a good one?*
As another Good Friday slips beneath
my increasingly agnostic radar
and the rat man introduces himself
by disclaiming the Easter Bunny.
That's not the whole of it of course.
When I pray in my fashion
it is still to the personal God of my childhood.
The one who spoke through all the rest:
through wrath and the gentling son
offered up as counterweight
good cop bad cop parenting
through all the magdalens
and their unregretted lives
the laughing Buddha
and all the prophets and saints
who might choose to return
their titles if they could, if we let them.

Through the elements too:
the wind that both fed and dispelled
my nightmares
tiny liberating fires of my own design
the earth I feared would one day bury me
but which has always held my imprint
as dearly as if I were its only child.
And the rain – obliterating, revivifying.
I suppose I'm with the actor who said
when asked about life after death
I have a shy hope…
So here it is – this grey shawl of a day
lightly embroidered
just so.

Tuesday Scrabble

With one of the best views of the lake
the ladies make cheat sheets and dictionaries
look dignified –
we play a player-assisted game
fingertips caressing the Lazy Susan.

It's not long before c gives *link*
a voice
and someone begins testing words
that just look right, really should be right.

If only *jus* were phonetic, if only *is*…
and what use *fuzz* and *fizz* without a blank.

A fisherwoman might think to add *p*
to *orgy* but it's enough on its own
to garner giggles, raise the bar.

arty stands briefly alone trying to stand out
before yielding to a *t* (fame by
association).

Others might decree you can't have it
if you can't pronounce it
use it sensibly in a sentence
say there are only so many lesser moves
worth making while waiting
that winning is its own reward.

But these players understand connection is all
how quickly the tiles can shift and fall.
Some victories better left to the imagination
(let the *i*'s think they have it).

When there's mention in parting
of another death in common, there it is
keenly felt in the backs of the calves
that woozy cliff-edge weakness
held in check until next Tuesday
when sure as swans' eggs they'll play again
strategically for fancy, never for keeps.

Quiet notes for friends

when you are too long away from certain friends
you risk being mistaken for someone else

Over four nights and three days nourished in obvious and startling ways. The scent of unwrapped, uneaten chocolate. The unspoken question volleyed, revelled in – how long can you live off delayed gratification? Fresh-frozen stroganoff for the impromptu kindred spirit. An Italian fish dish on a bread-bed laced with capers and anchovies. Raspberries gently cupped from the cane. Quiche and salted caramel tarts so badly good. Curry and ginger ale. Unfakable custard. Conversation changing lanes without needing to signal, each topic weighted with intrinsic value. From exercise bikes to goshawks. Historical to science fiction. At turns I find myself swapping recipes for ghost stories, doctrines for puns. Standing on one leg, arms out at my sides, eyes closed in a personal best test of balance and faith. One morning on a lone beach walk I discover a type of seaweed so closely resembling viscera, in the right mood I might find myself! There are bright helium laughs I could float away on and quiet notes so raw as to be both wound and balm. Inevitable I suppose given ages and temperaments that we should circle back to the duplicitous body; marshy, edgy, but really (we agree don't we?) unable to hold a candle to the rest. On my return an extra bag to make a meal of – Chinese cabbage and pods of green peas. And for my own potted patch: miner's lettuce, yellow zucchini seeds, talisman of oregano, the fidelity of rosemary, marjoram – favoured flower of Aphrodite. My blood zinging with poetic transfusion. Yes when you are too long away from such friends that old carapace which serves no one not even the friendless threatens to reinstall itself over your heart or soul or that piece of you anyway without which it is so much harder to believe in the part you've been given. This particular way of being seen and seeing.

Layers

When our neighbour moves out
it instantly becomes too late to take the relationship
to any next level, to inch beyond the suburban courtesies
of collected mail, watered plants, the odd borrowed thing –
to advance from fellow-tenant to confidante.
On occasion I glimpsed the safety rails of small talk
buckling, giving way to the crannies of deeper revelation
and once or twice it seemed we almost chanced it before
blinking back to the level surface of low-risk acquaintanceship.
How perfectly the kitchen window frames the pademelon.
Vital in this climate to dress to the conditions:
base layers, middle layers, shell layers.
The noise pollution of hoons comes with the territory.
When the professional cleaners back out of the shared driveway
all trace taken with them I surprise myself by texting
thank you for being the perfect neighbour
try to summon and hold back certain hallmarks of identity
hints at bigger story, from fading too quickly:
a seasonal asthmatic cough
whole meals dehydrated for camping
the happy birthday song sung twice
to the visiting niece of an ex-husband
the thinnest ribbon of smoke crossing balconies
its plummy scent carrying notes of lemon, apple, elsewhere…

My mother's daughter

Similarities in childhood masked
by the 24/7 business of working
toward that dream home/life
and a freezer large enough to maintain
the smaller miracle of loaves and chickens
though even this became part and parcel;
the frugality gene inherited and honed.

Early adolescence encouraged
separateness and mockery
strategic word placement floating
an illusion of knowledge.
What use then – 101 ways
to revitalise a marriage
of ground beef and cabbage.
How to temporarily shutter the heart
against permanent impairment.

Comparative photographs of us
in our 20s reveal more of a kinship:
the slight upturn of sun-kissed noses
shorter haircuts
and slighter frames
a suggestion that without wings
the imperative to run
is harder to turn from.

Skirting middle-age some traits
become almost untenable:
the warning jut of jaw
the little laugh before the lie.

Each morning in the mirror
as eyes assess skin's delicate hold
my mother's daughter greets me kindly
one more fold in the soul's origami.

Chiaroscuro

Sitting on the bund wall
arranging brushes and pallets
angles of limbs and line of sight.

Behind her the water in full sun
is a pristine mirror of cloud and bird
but the artist is fishing
for the light between shadows
where the spectrum lies softer, truer
against the thick soup of the lake
and the trails swans leave through reeds
are as worthy of attention
as the swans themselves.

Night stole her voice
but the morning is promising its return
sevenfold.

Framed by cliffs and overhangs she is held
in an ancient knowledge of elements
compelled by the way grey can tell the story
of a painting more faithfully
than any white backdrop.

Only later will she add her signature
aspects of bold reimagining
hinting at the unearthly
chroma beyond the pale.

Instant gratification

He would never admit
to an uncontrolled appetite for anything –
swapping one troubled country for another
dreams of freedom for dreams of fiefdom.
With so many children looking for counsel
he gave up tobacco as a matter of principle
and perhaps just in case it proved to be
the most he could do.
No more the drinker of his youth or middling years
these days a second beer at half-time
and an appetite for food proportionate
to aided daily walks and one-sided debates
with game show hosts.
Longevity finally in his corner
he draws the line at giving up butter or salt
battered fish and chips
soda bread farls fried in lard
the pure rapture of a Mars bar.
Though we never went without growing up
we always kept one eye on his plate
fought for the bacon rinds when he was done
sucking them bland.
Long before the disembodiment of the internet
the promise of fulfilment was always sensate;
olfaction, gustation.
We were led by the nose, held by the tongue.
In our daydreams the world before the word
was made to order, flavoured and textured
with no end in sight.

Hum and fray

What does it matter whether
we ignited in space
or crawled out from the sea
if such questions merely serve
to distract us
from our sense of belonging
from our active belonging.

By us of course I mean those
for whom wonder too readily
morphs into near-useless
analysis. Pass the petri dish.

Once we believed lemmings fell
from stormy skies
then
we got on with our days.

Now plagued by face values
we have become perilous
as these warming degrees of separation
as the rhino and the honeybee
as the sea turtle and her finite sons.

Still the world turns and us with it
every imbalance gravitating toward its centre
coaxing us into unthinking moments of awe
into nullifying indifference
and the imagined power it affords.

Hush...

humming at the edge of our senses
all the live wires of common existence
desirous and willing to reconnect.

Sulphur

Mid-spring, not yet
the winter of my self
but counting laps because
if not equal to the joy
of the walk itself
exercise has become
exercise.

I now recognise the speed
at which an hour or 24
can elude me

but today I stay the course
looking up as these anti-
musicians alert me
to transfiguration

to wonder as I write
at this rendering of being
in words – all approximations
and limitations.

Again and again beauty
belies any name I give it;
bucolic for instance
a word I cannot reconcile
with pleasantry of any kind
each time hearing bubonic
in its stead.

Now these cockatoos
sulphur-crested and signalling
my brain into a holding pattern
of uneasy connotations.
The reductive atomic number 16.
Brimstone's divine damnation.

And still I welcome this weirdly
softening buttercup sky
these raucous angels on L-plates
raining life's discordant truths
until I find once more
my own uncensored laugh
my own remarkable twist in the path.

Thrum

When we moved into the house next to the commercial
laundry next to the wholesale bakery on the busy road
I knew I wouldn't mind. The unfamiliar noises and smells
coincided with a growing belief that there can be such a thing
as too much peace and quiet though I was raised with the idea
there was nothing you wouldn't give for a bit of it. I had done
my time in various states of isolation which did me the good
of any medicine. Now each morning I wake to the hum of industry
all the whir and hiss, chugs and clunks and the world smells like
freshly pressed linen and hot cross buns as if it were in endless
preparation for the second coming. Maybe one day I will grow
weary of it as I did of the rippling calm but I'm not so sure.
At night the light display on the bedroom wall phasing
red, green, yellow – an unforeseen comfort as if designed to
hearten the alien cogs of my own being into joining the thrum.
There is a balcony out from the kitchen door ending in a small
triangle of earth and a corrugated-iron wall behind which
the clockwork cycles of washing and drying take place
now and then the muffled laughter of co-workers who may
have morphed into friends. Here I can sit on a wooden stool
in reach of the thorns wrestling the orange blossom and
an array of plants in pots at my feet: cherry tomatoes
spring onions, the native mint Poorinda David because
it contains the name of my brother long-gone and has survived
many transplants and much neglect, the four herbs of the song
and some radishes for kick. Sparrows freely come and go
from their nests in the guttering and there may be a rat or two
in the crawlspace below belonging no more or less than piston
and pump, drum and drain pipe, than the fans and gaskets
holding in check the quicksilver of our own desire spinning
as we are on this shared axis which for all the known worlds
feels like home.

www.ingramcontent.com/pod-product-compliance
Lightning Source LLC
Chambersburg PA
CBHW021130080526
44587CB00012B/1211